MEET THE CHICAGO BULLS

BY BRENDAN HANRAHAN

SCHOLASTIC INC.

New York   Toronto   London   Auckland   Sydney

Photo Credits:

Cover(Kukoc/Jordan), 7(left), 10(large), 11(Longley), 12(Harper), 14(Caffey), 25(Buechler), 28(lower right): NBA/Scott Cunningham. **Cover(Pippen), 4(bottom), 8, 9(both), 22(top), 24, 25(Jordan), 27(both), 28(Pippen), 30(trophy):** NBA/Nathaniel S. Butler. **3, 19(Rodman):** NBA/Bill Baptist. **4(top), 6, 14(Salley), 18, 26(left), 28(left), 29:** NBA/Barry Gossage. **5, 10(small inset), 17, 19(top), 22(Rodman):** NBA/Andrew D. Bernstein. **7(right), 26(right):** NBA/Richard Lewis. **11(Kukoc):** NBA/Ronald C. Modra. **12(Kerr), 22(Pippen):** NBA/Steve Woltman. **13(Wennington):** NBA/Sam Forencich. **13(Simpkins), 14(Brown):** NBA/Steve Di Paola. **14(Edwards/Buechler):** NBA/Gary Dineen. **14(Haley):** NBA/Chris Corvatta. **15, 23:** NBA/Jerry Wachter. **19(lower right), 20, 21(upper right):** NBA/Lou Capozzola. **21(upper left):** NBA/Jon Soohoo. **21(bottom), 30(Kemp), 31(top/bottom):** NBA/Andy Hayt. **22(Jordan):** NBA/Noren Trotman.

ISBN 0-590-97327-4

©1996 by NBA Properties, Inc.
All rights reserved. Published by Scholastic Inc.

12 11 10 9 8 7 6 5 4 3 2 1   6 7 8 9/9 0 1/0

Printed in the U.S.A.

First Scholastic printing, November 1996

Book Design: **Oberlander Design**

In **1995-96** the **Chicago Bulls** won their fourth championship in six years. But this was the most impressive of all. From November through June the Bulls ruled the NBA. They dominated as few teams ever have. With Michael Jordan once again at the top of his game, and Scottie Pippen displaying his considerable all-around skills, the Bulls were nothing short of **spectacular.** Throughout the season, records tumbled. And so did opponents. Night after night, the United Center rocked . . . and the **Bulls rolled.** But they were not always champions. . . .

The **Chicago** Bulls were born in 1966,

as an expansion team in the National Basketball Association. And, like most expansion teams, they lost more games than they won. Unlike the 1990's, when the Bulls became one of the most glamorous franchises in professional sports, the teams of the 1960's were decidedly blue collar. They worked hard on defense. They crashed the boards. Each night they put their hearts on the floor.

Still, success was slow to come. It wasn't until 1970-71 that the Bulls had their first winning season. But over the next five years they were one of the finest teams in the NBA. In fact, the Bulls won their first divisional title in 1975. That team featured **Chet Walker,** a forward who is now in the NBA Hall of Fame, and **Tom Boerwinkle,** the Bulls all-time leading rebounder. It also included a high-scoring forward named **Bob Love** and a slick point guard named **Norm Van Lier**. **Jerry Sloan,** now the coach of the Utah Jazz, was the team's defensive star.

With the arrival of **Michael Jordan** in 1984 the Bulls became a different kind of team. Michael brought grace and elegance to dusty old Chicago Stadium. He gave the Bulls style. He gave them wings.

What Michael could not give the Bulls was a title. At least, not by himself. He proved that he was the NBA's most explosive player by winning the first of his eight scoring titles in 1986-87. Michael averaged 37.1 points that year, but the Bulls failed to reach the .500 mark.

Soon, though, Michael found himself playing with a magnificent supporting cast. The Bulls used one of their first-round draft picks in 1987 on **Horace Grant,** a forward from Clemson. With the other they chose University of Virginia center Olden Polynice. But the player they really wanted was **Scottie Pippen,** a little-known forward from Central Arkansas who had already been drafted by the Seattle SuperSonics. So the Bulls traded Polynice and draft choices for Pippen.

It was a shrewd maneuver. Within three years Pippen was an NBA All-Star, and the Bulls were one of the best teams in the league. **Phil Jackson** became head coach before the 1989-90 season and led the Bulls to the Eastern Conference Finals.

Then, in 1990-91, everything came together. John Paxson, an unselfish player with a textbook jump shot, took some of the heat off Michael in the backcourt. Center **Bill Cartwright,** a 12-year veteran, played with the spirit and stamina of a kid. And Horace and Scottie became stars. The Bulls set a franchise record with 61 victories that season. They fell in love with Chicago Stadium all over again, winning 26 consecutive games at home. Best of all, they captured their **first NBA championship.**

But that was only the beginning. The Bulls won a **second** consecutive title in 1992. And a **third** in 1993. They played without Michael in 1993-94, yet still reached the Eastern Conference Finals. And in 1994-95 they reached the conference semifinals.

Michael returned for a full season in 1995-96, and with him came a sense of purpose. Michael is one of the most competitive athletes on the planet. He never settles for second best. He gives everything he has each day — even in practice. And he expects nothing less of his teammates.

So they rallied around him, and they became world champions again. In fact, they became more than just champions. They became a team that redefined the sport of professional basketball. The Bulls set an NBA **record** by winning **72 games** during the regular season. At their new home, the United Center, they were virtually unbeatable. They charged through the play-offs as if on a mission. In the finals they beat the Seattle SuperSonics, 4-2, prompting some people to suggest that the 1995-96 Bulls were one of the greatest teams in NBA history. A team that could stand proudly beside the most famous and successful teams the game has ever known: the 1966-67 **Philadelphia 76ers**; the 1971-72 **Los Angeles Lakers**; the 1982-83 **Philadelphia 76ers**; and the 1985-86 **Boston Celtics**.

The **1995-96 Bulls** were more than just Michael Jordan. They were a **team.** **Steve Kerr** and **Ron Harper** split time at one guard spot. Scottie Pippen proved he was one of the most versatile players in the game. Dennis Rodman and Luc Longley dominated the boards. Toni Kukoc was the best sixth man in the league.

The Bulls were a team without a weakness. They were a team of destiny. The challenge before them now is to win another title. To prove that their **greatness** can endure.

5

Michael leads the way

If the legend of Michael Jordan ended with his retirement in 1993, it would still have been the most splendid of NBA lore. Leading the Bulls to three straight titles, he grew famous for scoring with graceful drives to the hoop or while floating on air above the rim.

But his story didn't end there. After a sometimes frustrating return late in the 1994-1995 season, Michael came back in 1995-1996 to add a brilliant new chapter to his amazing career. It was a thrill just to see him on the floor again—knowing that on any night he might explode for 30, 40, 50 points or more.

As it turned out, 1995-1996 was a year for which Michael Jordan will always be remembered. He won a record eighth scoring title and was named the league's MVP a fourth time. After he thought he'd done it all, Michael came back and proved to the world he could do even more.

CAREER HIGHLIGHTS (Yeah, he's had a few.)

- Only player ever to win eight NBA scoring titles
- Highest career scoring average in NBA history, 32 ppg
- Bulls all-time leading scorer with 24,489 points
- NBA MVP: 1988, 1991, 1992, 1996
- NBA Finals MVP: 1991, 1992, 1993, and 1996 (only player ever to win the award four times)

- NBA All-Star Game MVP: 1988, 1996
- NBA All-Star: 1985-1993, 1996
- NBA Defensive Player of the Year: 1988
- NBA leader in steals: 1988, 1990, 1993
- NBA All-League: 1987-1993, 1995
- NBA All-Defense: 1988-1993, 1995
- NBA Rookie of the Year: 1985

MICHAEL JORDAN   NO. 23   EXPERIENCE: 11 YEARS

Position	Height/Weight	Birth Date	College
Guard	6'-6"/198 pounds	2/17/63	North Carolina '85

	GP	FG%	FT%	Rebs.	Asst.	Pts.	Avg.
1995-96:	82	.495	.834	543	352	2,491	30.4
Career:	766	.512	.844	4,879	4,377	24,489	32.0

Scottie does it all

Scottie Pippen and the Bulls have come a long way together since his rookie year, 1987-1988, when Michael Jordan first took him under his wing. With Michael's steady guidance, Scottie developed into a top scorer and rebounder, and made the Bulls a true play-off contender for the first time in years.

Since playing a leading role for the Bulls in each of their championships, Scottie is now known as perhaps the most complete player in the league. A member of six All-Star teams and five All-Defensive teams, Scottie Pippen does it all for the Bulls at both ends of the court.

DID YOU KNOW?

Scottie recorded an amazing seventeenth career triple-double in the first round of the playoffs against the Heat with 22 points, 18 rebounds, and 10 assists.

SCOTTIE PIPPEN   NO. 33   EXPERIENCE: 9 YEARS

Position	Height/Weight			Birth Date	College		
Forward	6'-7"/210 pounds			9/25/65	Central Arkansas '87		
	GP	FG%	FT%	Rebs.	Asst.	Pts.	Avg.
1995-96:	77	.463	.679	496	452	1,496	19.4
Career:	707	.486	.687	4,900	3,723	12,490	17.7

CAREER HIGHLIGHTS

- NBA All-Star Game MVP: 1994
- NBA All-Star: 1990, 1992-1996
- NBA All-Defensive Team: 1992-1996
- Member of 1992 and 1996 Olympic Dream Teams

SCOTTIE 33 PIPPEN

You never know what color his hair will be, but at least you can find Dennis Rodman in the same place every game. He'll be under the boards, pulling down rebounds like no other player in the NBA. Plain and simple, Dennis *wants* the ball.

In ten years with the Pistons, Spurs, and Bulls, Dennis has studied every shooter in the game. Dennis knows their spots, the arc they use, where they miss. It's that kind of know-how that earned him a fifth straight rebounding title in 1995-1996, to become the only player besides Wilt "The Stilt" Chamberlain to lead the league in rebounding with three different teams.

DID YOU KNOW?

Dennis wears number 91 for the Bulls, because 9 and 1 add up to 10, his number in high school, college, and in the NBA with the Pistons and Spurs.

"HAIR" MAN OF THE BOARDS

Year	Team	Total Rebs/Avg.
1986-1987	Pistons	332/4.3
1987-1988	Pistons	715/8.7
1988-1989	Pistons	772/9.4
1989-1990	Pistons	792/9.7
1990-1991	Pistons	1026/12.5
1991-1992	Pistons	1530*/18.7
1992-1993	Pistons	1132*/18.3
1993-1994	Spurs	1367*/17.3
1994-1995	Spurs	823*/16.8
1995-1996	Bulls	952*/14.9

* Led league in rebounding

DENNIS RODMAN   NO. 91   EXPERIENCE: 10 YEARS

Position	Height/Weight		Birth Date	College		
Forward	6'-8"/210 pounds		5/13/61	S. Oklahoma State '86		

	GP	FG%	FT%	Rebs.	Asst.	Pts.	Avg.
1995-96:	64	.480	.528	952	160	351	5.5
Career:	741	.535	.589	9,441	1,156	5,914	8.0

Since being drafted by the Timberwolves in 1991, Luc Longley has improved in each of his five years in the NBA. A native of Australia, he hit his stride after being traded to Chicago for Stacey King in 1994. Luc gives the Bulls tough interior defense. In addition, Luc continues to develop his offensive game, providing unexpected scoring punch throughout the season.

DID YOU KNOW?

Luc is a surprisingly good free-throw shooter for a big guy, knocking down nearly three of every four free throws he's been given in the NBA.

NGLEY   NO. 13   EXPERIENCE: 5 YEARS

Height/Weight			Birth Date		College	
7'-2"/265 pounds			1/19/69		New Mexico '91	
GP	FG%	FT%	Rebs.	Asst.	Pts.	Avg.
62	.482	.777	318	119	564	9.1
314	.466	.744	1,511	405	2,050	6.5

TONI 7 KUKOC

It was a dunk on Alonzo Mourning in the 1990 Goodwill Games that got the Bulls to notice Toni Kukoc. They kept an eye on him again at the '92 Olympics, when he led Croatia in the final against Michael, Scottie, and the original Dream Team. After that, the Bulls knew Toni Kukoc could play with the best players in the game. He was ready for the NBA.

Toni adjusted quickly to the NBA in 1993-1994, averaging nearly 11 points a game as a rookie. He's only improved over time. Scoring off the bench and starting while Scottie was hurt, Toni was an easy choice to win the NBA Sixth Man Award.

DID YOU KNOW?

Toni has been given all sorts of nicknames over his career, including "Pink Panther," "Alien," "The Spider of Split," "The Waiter," and "Kuki."

TONI KUKOC   NO. 7   EXPERIENCE: 3 YEARS

Position	Height/Weight			Birth Date		College	
Forward	6'-11"/233 pounds			9/18/68		Split, Croatia	
	GP	FG%	FT%	Rebs.	Asst.	Pts.	Avg.
1995-96:	81	.490	.772	323	287	1,065	13.1
Career:	237	.478	.755	1,060	911	3,150	13.3

RON 9 HARPER

The Bulls have relied on Ron Harper for his defense since he joined the team in '94, but he can score, too. Ron sank 22 points in a game against the Cavs last season to join Toni Kukoc as the only players besides Michael or Scottie to lead the Bulls in scoring in 1995-96.

RON HARPER	NO. 9	EXPERIENCE: 10 YEARS					
Position	**Height/Weight**			**Birth Date**	**College**		
Guard	6'-6"/198 pounds			1/20/64	Miami-Ohio '86		
	GP	**FG%**	**FT%**	**Rebs.**	**Asst.**	**Pts.**	**Avg.**
1995-96:	80	.467	.705	213	208	594	7.4
Career:	689	.451	.721	3,143	2,986	11,410	16.6

STEVE 25 KERR

It was Steve Kerr's accurate jump shot that first got him to the NBA in 1988. And that same fine shooting touch earned him a spot on the Bulls roster in 1993. The league's all-time three-point field goal percentage leader at .480, he's one shooter the Bulls can count on with the game on the line.

STEVE KERR	NO. 25	EXPERIENCE: 8 YEARS					
Position	**Height/Weight**			**Birth Date**	**College**		
Guard	6'-3"/180 pounds			9/27/65	Arizona '88		
	GP	**FG%**	**FT%**	**Rebs.**	**Asst.**	**Pts.**	**Avg.**
1995-96:	82	.506	.929	110	192	688	8.4
Career:	507	.489	.853	635	1,136	3,369	6.6

DICKEY SIMPKINS   NO. 8   EXPERIENCE: 2 YEARS

Position	Height/Weight			Birth Date	College	
Forward	6'-9"/248 pounds			4/6/72	Providence '94	
	GP	FG%	FT%	Rebs.	Asst.	Pts.	Avg.
1995-96:	60	.481	.629	156	38	216	3.6
Career:	119	.451	.657	307	75	422	3.5

Despite limited playing time his first two seasons, the Bulls hope Dickey Simpkins can become a force up front. Drafted in the first round of the '94 draft, Dickey has had to wait his turn to play behind Scottie and Dennis in 1995-1996, but continues to develop and grow as a player.

DICKEY 8 SIMPKINS

BILL WENNINGTON   NO. 34   EXPERIENCE: 9 YEARS

Position	Height/Weight			Birth Date	College	
Center	7'-0"/260 pounds			4/26/63	St. John's '85	
	GP	FG%	FT%	Rebs.	Asst.	Pts.	Avg.
1995-96:	71	.493	.860	174	46	376	5.3
Career:	566	.466	.780	1,841	361	2,697	4.8

Bill Wennington first made a name for himself in college as a steady, blue-collar type player for St. Johns—a great team that also featured Chris Mullin and Mark Jackson. After five years with the Mavericks and one with the Kings, Bill signed with the Bulls in the middle of the 1993-1994 season. He has provided strength, consistency, and clutch performances ever since.

BILL 34 WENNINGTON

JOHN 22 SALLEY

John won two NBA championships with the Pistons in 1989 and '90. He came to the Bulls in 1996 after stints with the Heat and Raptors.

JOHN SALLEY		NO. 22		EXPERIENCE: 10 YEARS		
Position	**Height/Weight**		**Birth Date**	**College**		
Forward	6'-11"/255 pounds		6/16/64	Georgia Tech '86		
	GP	**FG%**	**FT%**	**Rebs.**	**Asst.**	**Pts.**	**Avg.**
1995-96*:	42	.450	.694	140	54	185	4.4
Career:	703	.509	.714	3,291	890	5,157	7.3

*NBA total. Salley played 25 games with the Toronto Raptors in 1995-1996, and 17 games with the Chicago Bulls.

RANDY BROWN

RANDY BROWN		NO. 0		EXPERIENCE: 5 YEARS		
Position	**Height/Weight**		**Birth Date**	**College**		
Guard	6'-2"/191 pounds		5/22/68	New Mexico St. 91		
	GP	**FG%**	**FT%**	**Rebs.**	**Asst.**	**Pts.**	**Avg.**
1995-96:	68	.406	.609	66	73	185	2.7
Career:	327	.443	.672	567	594	1,534	4.7

A guard who came to the Bulls as a free agent after four seasons with the Kings, Randy reached a 1995-96 season high by scoring 16 points against the Pistons.

JASON 35 CAFFEY

A rookie selected by Chicago in the first round of the 1995 NBA Draft, Jason came off the bench to play in 57 games.

JASON CAFFEY		NO. 35			EXPERIENCE: ROOKIE	
Position	**Height/Weight**		**Birth Date**	**College**		
Forward	6'-8"/255 pounds		6/12/73	Alabama '95		
	GP	**FG%**	**3FG%**	**FT%**	**Rebs.**	**Asst.**	**Pts.**	**Avg.**
1995-96	57	.438	.000	.588	111	24	182	3.2

JUD 30 BUECHLER

JUD BUECHLER		NO. 30		EXPERIENCE: 6 YEARS		
Position	**Height/Weight**		**Birth Date**	**College**		
Forward	6'-6"/220 pounds		6/19/68	Arizona '90		
	GP	**FG%**	**FT%**	**Rebs.**	**Asst.**	**Pts.**	**Avg.**
1995-96:	74	.463	.636	111	56	278	3.8
Career:	339	.449	.651	629	290	1340	4.0

Versatile enough to play at the forward and guard positions, Jud joined the Bulls in 1994 after playing with the Nets, Spurs, and Warriors.

JACK 54 HALEY

Jack returned to Chicago in 1995 for the first time since his rookie season, 1988-1989. In between, he played with the Nets and Lakers. Jack was Dennis Rodman's teammate and best friend on the Spurs for two seasons.

JACK HALEY		NO. 54		EXPERIENCE: 8 YEARS		
Position	**Height/Weight**		**Birth Date**	**College**		
Center	6'-10"/242 pounds		1/27/64	UCLA '87		
	GP	**FG%**	**FT%**	**Rebs.**	**Asst.**	**Pts.**	**Avg.**
1995-96:	1	.333	.500	2	0	5	5.0
Career:	305	.430	.656	875	77	1118	3.7

JAMES 53 EDWARDS

JAMES EDWARDS		NO. 53		EXPERIENCE: 19 YEARS		
Position	**Height/Weight**		**Birth Date**	**College**		
Center	7'-1"/252 pounds		11/22/55	Washington '77		
	GP	**FG%**	**FT%**	**Rebs.**	**Asst.**	**Pts.**	**Avg.**
1995-96:	28	.373	.615	40	11	98	3.5
Career:	1168	.495	.698	6,004	1,499	14,862	12.7

An NBA veteran whose 19 years of experience ranks him with Kareem Abdul-Jabbar (20 years). James has played for seven different NBA teams and won NBA championships with the Pistons in 1989 and '90.

The Coach—Phil Jackson

Phil Jackson knows he's one guy on the Bulls bench who can't put points on the board. It's the coach's job to show the players how to win games and since 1989 no one's done that better than Phil.

He doesn't prowl sidelines screaming orders. Phil has a calmer style. His last words to Michael Jordan in the 1991 Finals were "Who's open?" It was all Michael had to hear to pass to John Paxson, who calmly buried a deep shot to win the title.

Phil worked magic again in 1995-1996, getting Michael, Scottie, Dennis, and the Bulls to come together and form perhaps the greatest team ever. It won him the Red Auerbach award for Coach of the Year and the respect of many as one of the all-time great coaches.

CAREER HIGHLIGHTS

- 1996 Red Auerbach award for Coach of the Year
- Bulls all-time winningest coach
- First coach to win championships in both the NBA (1991, 1992, 1993, 1996) and CBA (1984)
- Ninth ever to win NBA championships as both a player (with the New York Knicks) and a coach

JAX FACTS

- Phil sometimes takes his dog, a golden retriever named Bo, to practice with him.
- Phil vacationed in a Native American tepee a few summers ago with one of his sons.
- Phil loves the music of The Grateful Dead.
- Phil averaged 6.7 points per game in 13 seasons in the NBA with the Knicks and Nets.
- Phil rode his bike from his New York City apartment to Madison Square Garden when the Knicks were home. On the road, he roomed with future Hall of Famer and United States Senator Bill Bradley.

THE BEST EVER?

Coach	W	L	Pct.
PHIL JACKSON	414	160	.721
Pat Riley*	798	339	.702
Billy Cunningham	698	454	.698
K. C. Jones	522	252	.674
Red Auerbach	938	479	.662
Rick Adelman*	327	200	.620
Lester Harrison	295	181	.620
Tom Heinsohn	427	263	.619
Jerry Sloan*	513	341	.601
Chuck Daly	564	379	.598

* Active coach

PHIL JACKSON

Date	Opp.	Score	Record
11/3	**HORNETS**	W 105-91	1-0

Bulls cruise as Michael Jordan opens the season scoring 42 points.

11/4	**CELTICS**	W 107-85	2-0

Scottie Pippen's 21 points lead the way.

11/7	**RAPTORS**	W 117-108	3-0

Michael leads the Bulls on decisive 15-0 second half run.

11/9	**CAVS**	W 106-88	4-0

Scottie notches a triple double with 8 points, 13 rebounds, and 12 assists.

11/11	**BLAZERS**	W 110-106	5-0

The Bulls remain the NBA's only undefeated team.

11/14	**MAGIC**	L 88-94	5-1

The always tough Magic give the Bulls their first loss of the season.

11/15	**CAVS**	W 113-94	6-1

The Bulls lead the whole way against the winless Cavaliers. Scottie nets 27 points.

11/17	**NETS**	W 109-94	7-1

Toni Kukoc drains 19 points to become the only player besides Michael or Scottie to lead the Bulls in scoring.

11/21	**MAVS**	W 108-102 (OT)	8-1

Michael's 36 points help seal the win in overtime.

11/22	**SPURS**	W 103-94	9-1

David Robinson scores 26 points for the Spurs, but Michael responds with 38 of his own.

11/24	**JAZZ**	W 90-85	10-1

Michael leads the Bulls with 34 points while John Stockton of the Jazz hits for 23.

11/26	**SONICS**	L 92-97	10-2

Luc Longley sinks a career-high 21 points, but it's not enough as the Sonics' Gary Payton and Shawn Kemp combine for 51 points.

11/27	**BLAZERS**	W 107-104	11-2

Michael scores 33 points while Scottie adds 21 points and 10 assists.

11/30	**GRIZZLIES**	W 94-88	12-2

The Grizzlies Greg Anthony keeps this one close by scoring 27 points.

12/2	**CLIPPERS**	W 104-98	13-2

The Bulls end a 7-game road trip and head home with the best record in the NBA.

A SEASON

For the **Chicago** Bulls, the 1995-1996 regular season was **one** for the record books. From the opening tap to the final buzzer, the **Bulls** dominated their opponents like no other team in NBA history.

It was a **team** effort. Scottie Pippen slashed, passed, and scored. Dennis Rodman once again proved he was the best pound-for-pound rebounder in the NBA. And Michael was Michael: simply the **best** basketball player on the planet.

Supporting players made important contributions, too. Steve Kerr knocked down **big shots** . . . Toni Kukoc provided scoring punch off the bench . . . Luc Longley added muscle inside . . . while Ron Harper seemed to do whatever the team needed on a nightly basis.

What follows is the **season in pictures** — a season of high-flying dunks, spectacular shots, fierce rebounding, and suffocating defense — and a complete, game-by-game review of the **greatest** season in NBA history.

FOR THE AGES

MICHAEL JORDAN —
A STEP AHEAD OF
THE COMPETITION.

Date	Opp.	Score	Record
12/6	**KNICKS**	W 101-94	14-2

A healthy Dennis Rodman returns to snare 20 rebounds.

12/8	**SPURS**	W 106-87	15-2

In his second game back, Dennis grabs a season high 21 rebounds.

12/9	**BUCKS**	W 118-106	16-2

Michael scores 45 points.

12/13	**MAGIC**	W 112-103	17-2

Michael outguns Penny Hardaway 36 points to 26 and the Bulls prevail.

12/14	**HAWKS**	W 127-108	18-2

Scottie breaks a 15-15 tie with a thundering dunk and the Bulls never look back.

12/16	**LAKERS**	W 108-88	19-2

Scottie scores 33 points to push the Bulls past Cedric Ceballos (27 points) and the Lakers.

12/18	**CELTICS**	W 123-114	20-2

Michael and Scottie combine for an incredible 74 points.

12/19	**MAVS**	W114-101	21-2

The Bulls outclass the injury-depleted Mavs.

12/22	**RAPTORS**	W113-104	22-2

Michael scores 27 pts. and grabs 10 rebounds.

12/23	**JAZZ**	W100-86	23-2

The Bulls tie a team record, winning 13 games in a row (set by the 1991-92 Bulls).

12/26	**PACERS**	L97-103	23-3

Reggie Miller and Mark Jackson hit critical three-point bombs to hand the Bulls their third loss.

12/29	**PACERS**	W120-93	24-3

Michael scores 29 points and Dennis grabs 16 rebounds. The Bulls get even with the Pacers.

12/30	**HAWKS**	W95-93	25-3

Dennis "The Worm" squirms for 21 rebounds for the third time this season.

1/3	**ROCKETS**	W100-86	26-3

The Bulls are a perfect 16-0 at home after beating Hakeem and the Rockets at the United Center and Scottie is named December's Player of the Month.

1/4	**HORNETS**	W117-93	27-3

Michael collects 27 points, 5 assists, and 5 rebounds despite sitting out the fourth quarter.

1/6	**BUCKS**	W113-84	28-3

Michael scores 32 points.

1/10	**SONICS**	W113-87	29-3

The Bulls avenge their loss by trouncing the Sonics.

1/13	**SIXERS**	W120-93	30-3

Michael takes rookie Jerry Stackhouse to school and buries a season high 48 points.

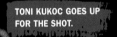

TONI KUKOC GOES UP FOR THE SHOT.

CHAEL AND MAGIC JOHNSON —
WO LEGENDS GO HEAD-TO-HEAD.

DENNIS RODMAN
DOES MORE
THAN REBOUND.

MICHAEL JORDAN:
NO PAIN, NO GAIN.

AMAZING MICHAEL.

Date	Opp.	Score	Record

1/15 BULLETS W116-109 31-3

Michael nets 46, tallying an incredible two-game total of 94 points.

1/16 SIXERS W116-104 32-3

Dennis Rodman dominates the boards with 21 rebounds.

1/18 RAPTORS W92-89 33-3

Raptors' rookie sensation Damon Stoudamire keeps this one close, scoring 26 points.

1/21 PISTONS W111-96 34-3

Michael scores 36 points to average 41 for his last four games.

1/23 KNICKS W99-79 35-3

The Bulls manhandle their old play-off rivals.

1/24 GRIZZLIES W104-84 36-3

The Bulls skin the Grizzlies.

1/26 HEAT W102-80 37-3

The Bulls win their 27th straight at home, breaking a record set by the 1992-93 team.

1/28 SUNS W93-82 38-3

The Bulls keep rolling on to a stunning 38-3 record.

1/30 ROCKETS W98-87 39-3

The Bulls become only the 9th team in NBA history to register a perfect month, going 14-0 in January.

2/1 KINGS W105-85 40-3

The Bulls break the record set by the 1971-72 Lakers for the best start in league history.

2/2 LAKERS W99-84 41-3

The Bulls beat the Lakers to win their ninth straight road game.

2/4 NUGGETS L99-105 41-4

The Bulls battle back from a 31-point deficit, but Mahmoud Abdul Rauf's last minute bucket gives Denver the victory. Win streak ends at 18.

2/6 SUNS L96-106 41-5

It's all Charles Barkley (35 points) down the stretch as the Bulls lose two in a row for the first time this season.

2/7 WARRIORS W99-95 42-5

Bulls get healthy. Michael scores 40 points.

2/13 BULLETS W111-98 43-5

The Bulls notch their 30th straight regular season home win.

2/15 PISTONS W112-109(OT) 44-5

A Dennis Rodman tip-in with less than a second left sends it to OT. Michael takes over from there.

2/16 T'WOLVES W103-100 45-5

Michael scores 35 points and Dennis grabs 19 rebounds to offset 29 points by the Wolves Isiah Rider.

SCOTTIE JAMS OVER
VLADE DIVAC.

SCOTTIE PIPPEN CONSULTS
WITH RON HARPER.

DENNIS AND
KARL MALONE HIT
THE HARDWOOD.

2/18 PACERS W110-102 46-5

Scottie Pippen scores 40 points and Michael adds 44 more as they become the first Bulls teammates, and only the ninth pair in NBA history, to score over 40 points in the same game.

2/20 CAVS W102-76 47-5

Ron Harper points the way by scoring a team-high 22 points.

2/22 HAWKS W96-91 48-5

A pair of Rodman free throws seal the victory in the final four seconds.

2/23 HEAT L104-112 48-6

Rex Chapman leads the Heat, scoring 39 pts. The Bulls pick up only their sixth loss.

2/25 MAGIC W111-91 49-6

The bench leads the Bulls to victory behind Toni Kukoc's 24 points, outscoring the Magic bench 41-4.

2/27 T'WOLVES W120-99 50-6

The Bulls reach 50 wins more quickly than any team in the history of pro sports in North America.

3/1 WARRIORS W110-87 51-6

Toni Kukoc's hot streak continues as he sinks 9 of 15 shots, including 4 of 7 three-pointers, to score 23 points in 24 minutes.

3/2 CELTICS W107-75 52-6

Dana Barros leads the hapless Celtics with only 12 pts. as the Bulls control throughout.

3/5 BUCKS W115-106 53-6

The Bucks never get closer than 8 points.

3/7 PISTONS W102-81 54-6

Michael scores an incredible 53 points. Scottie dishes 10 assists.

3/10 KNICKS L72-104 54-7

Patrick Ewing (26 points, 14 rebounds) leads the Knicks on a 34-6 run in the second half. Bulls score a season low 72 points.

3/13 BULLETS W103-86 55-7

Scottie Pippen's consecutive game streak ends as back and knee pain force him to sit. Toni Kukoc and Luc Longley step up to score 16 points each.

3/15 NUGGETS W108-87 56-7

Toni Kukoc passes for 10 assists.

3/16 NETS W97-93 57-7

Dennis Rodman is suspended for seven games for head-butting a referee.

3/18 SIXERS W98-94 58-7

Without Scottie or the Worm, the Bulls barely hang on to get Coach Phil Jackson his 400th career win.

3/19 KINGS W89-67 59-7

The Bulls remain invincible at home with a perfect 33-0 record.

DENNIS BATTLES DAVID ROBINSON UNDER THE BOARDS.

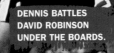

SCOTTIE GOES UP AGAINST RICK SMITS.

MICHAEL SHOOTS.

MICHAEL SOARS.

■ Michael was only the third player chosen in the 1984 NBA Draft. The Bulls chose him after the Houston Rockets took Hakeem Olajuwon first and the Portland Trail Blazers chose Sam Bowie second. Charles Barkley was drafted fifth that year, by the Philadelphia 76ers.

■ Michael scored his first bucket for the Bulls banking in a 12-footer in the first quarter of a game against the Bullets on opening night, October 26, 1984.

■ Michael has scored 40 or more points against every team in the NBA.

■ Michael keeps his shoes from his most memorable games.

■ Michael loved playing in the Bulls old arena, the Chicago Stadium, because he said the baskets seemed bigger there.

■ Michael's number 23 was retired by the Bulls on November 1, 1994, in a ceremony at the United Center. It had been worn by seven Bulls players, including Norm Van Lier (1971-1978).

■ Michael was twice named college basketball Player of the Year while playing for the University of North Carolina.

■ Michael always wears his old UNC shorts under his Bulls uniform for good luck.

■ Michael first dunked in a game at age 14, playing for Virgo Junior High in Wilmington, North Carolina, in 1977. He was 5 feet 10.

■ Michael has been afraid of the water since he was seven and a friend of his drowned while they were swimming in the ocean.

Date	Opp.	Score	Record
3/21	**KNICKS**	W107-86	60-7

The Bulls new acquisition John Salley (12 points, 8 rebounds) pays immediate dividends.

3/24	**RAPTORS**	L108-109	60-8

Toronto's Damon Stoudamire nails 30 points. Steve Kerr loses a chance to pull it out when his shot clangs off the rim.

3/28	**HAWKS**	W111-80	61-8

Regulars rest as the Hawks shoot poorly.

3/30	**CLIPPERS**	W106-85	62-8

Scottie Pippen leads the Bulls with 22 points.

4/2	**HEAT**	W110-92	63-8

Dennis Rodman grabs 13 rebounds. Michael and Scottie score 32 points each. Toni Kukoc adds 17.

4/4	**HEAT**	W100-92	64-8

Michael becomes only the 4th player in NBA history to reach 2,000 career steals. Toni Kukoc scores a career high 34 points.

4/5	**HORNETS**	W126-92	65-8

Scottie Pippen scores 28 points and snares 14 rebounds.

4/7	**MAGIC**	W90-86	66-8

Horace Grant's jumper with a minute to go, followed by Michael's game winner seconds later, brings this nail-biter to a stunning finish.

4/8	**HORNETS**	L97-98	66-9

The Hornets end Chicago's NBA record home win streak at 44 regular season games.

4/11	**NETS**	W113-100	67-9

Six Bulls finish in double figures and the team never trails.

4/12	**SIXERS**	W112-82	68-9

The Bulls sweep the sorry Sixers.

4/14	**CAVS**	W98-72	69-9

The Bulls win in Cleveland to notch a team record 31 road victories.

4/16	**BUCKS**	W86-80	70-9

Luc Longley's two free throws in the final seconds clinch an NBA record 70 wins. The Lakers won 69 games in 1971-72, a record that stood for 27 years.

4/18	**PISTONS**	W110-79	71-9

Michael rests for much of the game. Backup Randy Brown scores a career high 16 points.

4/20	**PACERS**	L99-100	71-10

Rik Smits scores 17 points as the Pacers become the only team to beat Chicago twice this season.

4/21	**BULLETS**	W103-93	72-10

The Bulls close out with 72 wins, as Michael Jordan earns his eighth scoring title, also an NBA record. The Bulls thoughts turn to the play-offs . . . and championship rings.

JED BUECHLER GOES VERTICAL.

MICHAEL DISHES TO THE OPEN MAN.

BUECHLER
30

LUC LONGLEY AND PATRICK EWING GO FOR THE BALL.

BULLS

THE 1 ROUND

The Bulls sweep 'Zo and Miami, 3-0.

COOLING OFF THE HEAT

MIAMI HEAT COACH, PAT RILEY.

MICHAEL CHALLENGES ALONZO MOURNING.

The Heat finished the first half of Game 1 with the Bulls tied at 54, but it was all downhill from there. The only real scare for the Bulls came when Michael strained his back in Game 2. But Michael bounced back in Game 3 to lead the Bulls in scoring, while Scottie helped extinguish the Heat with his seventeenth career triple-double.

The Knicks came in grimly determined, but it was the Bulls who came up big at critical moments. Scottie's monster dunk led the charge in Game 2 and Michael put Game 3 into overtime by sinking a three; but the unlikely hero of this series was Bill Wennington. His two buckets broke the Knicks in Game 4 and set the Bulls up to win the series in Game 5.

NECK &NECK WITH THE KNICKS

THE 2ND ROUND

The Bulls overcome Patrick Ewing and the Knicks, 4-1.

PATRICK EWING CLASHES WITH TONI KUKOC.

SCOTTIE AND CHARLES OAKLEY GET PHYSICAL.

Game 1 / May 5	BULLS 91–Knicks 84
Game 2 / May 7	BULLS 91–Knicks 80
Game 3 / May 11	KNICKS 102–Bulls 99 (OT)
Game 4 / May 12	Bulls 94–KNICKS 91
Game 5 / May 14	BULLS 94–Knicks 81
Home team in CAPS	

THE CONFERENCE

Bulls put a spell on Magic.

The Bulls faced the Orlando **Magic** in a repeat of the 1995 Eastern Conference Finals. But so much had changed in one year. In the 1995 series the Bulls did not have Dennis Rodman. And Michael Jordan had only recently returned to the NBA. The Magic, meanwhile, were one of the most talented young teams in the league. And they were hungry.

This time, though, the Bulls would not be denied.

PHIL CONGRATULATES SCOTTIE FOR A JOB WELL DONE.

MICHAEL GETS READY TO JUMP INTO THE FRAY.

Had the Magic been at full strength, perhaps it might have been a more competitive series. But luck was not on their side. Horace Grant aggravated an elbow injury in **Game 1** and missed the rest of the series. Brian Shaw went down in **Game 2**, and Nick Anderson was hurt in **Game 3**. The patched-up unit that faced the Bulls was not nearly as strong as the team that had won 60 games during the regular season.

The series was anything but the dream matchup some observers had predicted. **The Bulls simply overwhelmed the Magic.** Dennis and Luc Longley made life miserable for Shaquille O'Neal on the boards. Michael and Scottie were magnificent. From the opening tip, the Bulls played the type of aggressive defense that had become their trademark. They allowed an average of just 84.8 points and swept the Magic, 4-0.

LUC CONTESTS SHAQ'S JUMP HOOK.

28

FINALS

GAME 1 / May 19   BULLS 121–Magic 83
GAME 2 / May 21   BULLS 93–Magic 88
GAME 3 / May 25   Bulls 86–MAGIC 67
GAME 4 / May 27   Bulls 106–MAGIC 101
Home team in CAPS

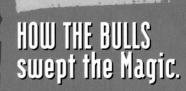

DISAPPEARING ACT

HOW THE BULLS swept the Magic.

● Dennis Rodman had a magnificent series. In addition to leading the Bulls in rebounding, he averaged 11.5 points, more than twice his season average.

● In each game the Magic had trouble handling the Bulls' defensive pressure, especially in the second half.

● The Magic relied too heavily on their star players, Shaquille O'Neal and Penny Hardaway. During the regular season Orlando had a neatly balanced offense. Because of injuries, though, Shaq and Penny were forced to carry more of the load against the Bulls. They accounted for 62 percent of the Magic's points.

● The Bulls were able to stop Orlando's long-range attack. Nick Anderson and Dennis Scott combined for just six three-point field goals.

● The Bulls owned the boards, especially after Horace Grant went down. Grant had averaged 9 rebounds a game during the 1995-96 season. With him on the bench, the Bulls out-rebounded the Magic, 182-123.

● Michael once again performed like the greatest player in the history of the game, especially in clutch situations. When the Bulls needed him most, in Game 4, he scored 45 points!

SCOTTIE RUNS
INTO A BLUE

THE NBA FINALS
That CHAMPIONSHIP Feeling!

A funny thing happened on the Bulls triumphant march to the championship ceremony.

As expected, the Bulls won the first three games of the NBA Finals. The champagne was put on ice. The trophy, polished and waiting, was stored in a nearby room. And the brooms came out, as nearly every fan anticipated a sweep. But somebody forgot to tell the Seattle SuperSonics.

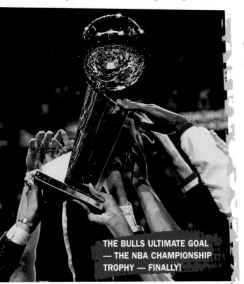

THE BULLS ULTIMATE GOAL — THE NBA CHAMPIONSHIP TROPHY — FINALLY!

The Sonics beat the Bulls in Game 4 — convincingly. Then the raging Bulls lost again. Two in a row! The series moved back to Chicago. For the first time all season, **things got serious**.

In fact, it shouldn't have surprised anyone. The Seattle SuperSonics, at 64-18, came into the play-offs with the 10th best regular-season record in NBA history. Led by the All-Star talents of Shawn Kemp and Gary Payton, the Sonics were good. Even great. And they weren't going to roll over for anybody.

But the Bulls reestablished control of the series in Game 6, at Chicago's United Center, a riotous arena where the Bulls just don't lose. In the end, the Bulls won their fourth championship in six years. Michael Jordan was named MVP of the NBA Finals for a fourth time. The magnificent season was complete. From beginning to end, the Bulls were the best. And now they had championship rings to prove it.

SERIES MVP
Michael Jordan

GAME 1
June 5   BULLS 107, Sonics 90

Michael came out with a scowl on his face: a bad sign for the Sonics. Five Bulls scored in double figures, offsetting Shawn Kemp's valiant 32-point effort. Toni Kukoc gave the Bulls a huge lift when he scored ten straight Chicago points to start the fourth quarter. Another key: Ron Harper held Gary Payton to only 13 points.

GAME ONE HERO: Toni Kukoc

GAME 2
June 7   BULLS 92, Sonics 88

It wasn't a thing of beauty, but the Bulls got the job done. Chicago dominated the boards, 65-46. Dennis Rodman snared 20 rebounds and generally made life miserable for the struggling Sonics. Michael contributed 29 points, while Scottie chipped in his second consecutive 21-point effort.

GAME TWO HERO: Dennis Rodman

GAME 3
June 9   Bulls 108, SONICS 86

The Bulls put on a clinic, a textbook example of how the game should be played. Chicago raced to a 19-4 lead in the first quarter, silencing the stunned Seattle home crowd. By halftime the Bulls led 62-38, and the second half was a mere formality. Luc Longley dominated the lane and scored 19 points. Toni Kukoc, starting for injured Ron Harper, tallied 14 points, 7 rebounds, and 7 assists. Michael scored 36.

GAME THREE HERO: Michael Jordan

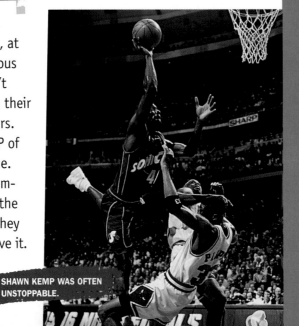

SHAWN KEMP WAS OFTEN UNSTOPPABLE.

Bulls Sink Sonics in Six!

SCOTTIE FALTERED ON TWO SPRAINED ANKLES.

GARY PAYTON ON ANOTHER THRILLING DRIVE TO THE HOOP.

GAME 4

June 12   SONICS 107, Bulls 86

Inspired by the return of injured team captain Nate McMillan, the Sonics finally looked like the team that had won 64 games in the regular season. The smothering, attacking Sonic defense disrupted Chicago's vaunted triangle offense. Shawn Kemp shot 12 for 17, scored 25 points, and grabbed 11 boards. Gary Payton played tough defense on Michael and notched 21 points, 11 assists. Scottie Pippen, playing on two sprained ankles, scored 9 points, hitting only 4 of 17 shots.

GAME FOUR HERO: **Gary Payton**

GAME 5

June 14   SONICS 89, Bulls 78

Michael scored 26, but the supporting cast never showed up. Want stats? While Michael hit 11 for 22 from the field, the rest of the Bulls were an awful 18 for 55. Worse yet, the Bulls shot a horrendous 3 for 26 from behind the arc. For the Sonics, a balanced team effort (Kemp 22, Payton 21, Hawkins 21, Schrempf 13) and renewed intensity did the trick. The Bulls clearly missed injured Ron Harper.

GAME FIVE HERO: **Shawn Kemp**

GAME 6

June 16   BULLS 87, Sonics 75

Strong rebounding and relentless defense undid the Sonics, as Dennis Rodman rose to the occasion with yet another clutch performance (19 boards). Scottie Pippen recovered from his shooting woes with a brilliant all-around game: 17 points, 8 rebounds, 5 assists, 4 steals. A victorious Michael Jordan, choked with emotion, dedicated the victory to his father: "This was for Dad."

GAME SIX HERO: **Dennis Rodman**

Home team in CAPS

THE BULLS ALL-TIME LEADERS*

CAREER

GAMES

Michael Jordan	766
Scottie Pippen	707
Jerry Sloan	684
John Paxson	645
Tom Boerwinkle	635

TOTAL POINTS

Michael Jordan	24,489
Bob Love	12,623
Scottie Pippen	12,490
Jerry Sloan	10,233
Chet Walker	9,788

ASSISTS

Michael Jordan	4,377
Scottie Pippen	3,723
Norm Van Lier	3,676
Reggie Theus	2,472
John Paxson	2,153

REBOUNDS

Tom Boerwinkle	5,745
Jerry Sloan	5,385
Artis Gilmore	5,342
Scottie Pippen	4,900
Horace Grant	4,721

THE BULLS REGULAR SEASON INDIVIDUAL RECORD HOLDERS

MOST POINTS
69 Michael Jordan
(vs. Cleveland, March 28, 1990)

MOST FIELD GOALS
27 Michael Jordan
(vs. Orlando, Jan. 16, 1993)

MOST FREE THROWS
26 Michael Jordan
(vs. New Jersey, Feb. 26, 1987)

MOST REBOUNDS
37 Tom Boerwinkle
(vs. Phoenix, Jan. 8, 1990)

MOST OFFENSIVE REBOUNDS
18 Charles Oakley
(vs. Milwaukee, March 15, 1986)

MOST DEFENSIVE REBOUNDS
25 Artis Gilmore
(vs. San Antonio, Dec. 22, 1978)

MOST ASSISTS
24 Guy Rodgers
(vs. New York, Dec. 21, 1966)

MOST TECHNICAL FOULS
3 Dick Motta
(vs. Boston, Oct. 29, 1968)

LONGEST SHOT:
84 feet Norm Van Lier
(vs. San Antonio, Jan. 19, 1977)

MOST BLOCKED SHOTS
12 Nate Thurmond
(vs. Atlanta, Oct. 18, 1974)

MOST CONSECUTIVE FIELD GOALS
11 Clem Haskins
(vs. Detroit, Feb. 15, 1970)